The Right Career

The Right Career

A Dictionary, Exploring Over
700 Career Jobs and Occupations
Around the World for Young Readers

Delois Pippen

To order additional copies of this book, contact:
Xlibris Corporation
1-888-795-4274
www.Xlibris.com
Orders@Xlibris.com
34404

DEDICATION

This book is dedicated to my husband Billie: My three children: Patrick, Cedric and La Tonya. To my mom, Lucille, my sister, Lois Jean and my beautiful granddaughters.

Welcome to The Right Career

A Dictionary, Exploring Over 700 Career Jobs and Occupations Around
The World for Young Readers.

There are many jobs and occupations whom we come in contact during our time on this earth. Some are temporary and some are for a lifetime. Some touch, the deepest part of our minds and souls. While others only scratch the surface of our life.

As children we have encounted family members with career changes growing up. We have seen how they bounced back with another job. We have seen family members make poor choices in selecting jobs and occupations. While others excel in their careers and live extraordinary. Some young people start out at age four, training to be successful. Such as golfers, musicians, dancers, singers etc. An early start, make a difference in your life.

Young readers please allow this book to become a tool for you during your journey in choosing your career. There are over 700 careers, jobs and occupations to choose from. With short definitions explaining each career to encourage you to prepare for tomorrow with the right choices. Every one has the potential to become successful in life, even if there are setbacks in life. If you can imagine it, you can achieve it. If you can dream it, you can become it!

Be Prepared In Life For The Unexpected!

"Plan A" may not work.
Prepare for "Plan B" in advance.

Acknowledgements

I would like to thank Xlibris Publisher for their outstanding work in editing my manuscript. Their service made my book much more professional and helped me relax just knowing that everything was in order. Thank you Xlibris for enable me to explore over 700 interesting careers, to help young readers choose a rewarding career path.

I'm so grateful for all my students of Noble Elementary School, Hamburg, Arkansas. The past thirty-six years, you've made a difference in my life. Never shall I forget the days spent on family careers and jobs.

A

accountant (ac-coun-tant): one who is in business to keep or examine books for mercantile.

acrobat trainer (ac-ro-bat train-er): one skilled in teaching muscular strength and coordination in walking.

activist (ac-tiv-ist): one with a doctrine or practice that emphasizes direct vigorous action especially in support of or opposition to one side of a controversial issue.

actor (ac-tor): a male player on stage in motion pictures.

actress (ac-tress): a woman who acts in movies and on stage.

actuary (ac-tu-ary): a statistician who calculates and states risks, premium for insurance, etc.

administrator (ad-min-is-tra-tor): one who manages or has charge of functions, schools, workforce, etc.

advertising serviceman (ad-ver-tis-ing, ser-vice): one who assists in communication, publicizing goods and commodity to the public.

advisor (ad-vis-or): one who gives advice such as a teacher in a school or college. One who counsels college students about their studies or career.

aerialist (ae-ri-al-ist) : one who performs on tightropes or trapezes at circus.

aerologist (aer-ol-o-gist): one who studies the atmosphere and its phenomena.

aeronaut (aero-naut): one who pilots a balloon.

aerospace engineer (aero-space en-gi-neer): one who studies professionally how to deal with aircraft manufacture, maintenance, and testing.

aerospace medicine man (aero-space med-i-cine man): one who studies medicine that deals with spaceflight.

agriculturist (ag-ri-cul-tur-ist): an expert in farming and raising livestock.

aide (aide): one who assists or helps other workers. A nurse or teacher aide.

air condition and heating salesperson (air-con-di-tion and heat-ing sales per-son): one who sells and repairs air-conditioning and heating units.

allergist (al-ler-gist): a specialist in diagnosis and treatment of allergies.

alpinist (al-pin-ist): one who mountain climbs in the Alps or other high mountains.

ambassador (am-bas-sa-dor): a dipomatic appointed as a messenger by the government.

ambulance attendant (am-bu-lance at-ten-dant): one who attends to sick patients in a special vehicle equipped for caring the sick and wounded, in taking them to the hospital.

annalist (an-nal-ist): one who keeps records of events in order, year by year, history of records.

anatomist (anat-o-mist): one skilled in anatomy, the structure of plants and animal parts.

anecdotist (an-ec-dot-ist): one who collects, publishes, or tells anecdotes.

anesthetist (anes-the-tist): one who is trained to give anesthetics.

anthropologist (an-thro-pol-o-gist): one skilled in science treating physical character and cultural development of man, including his origin, evolution, customs, and beliefs.

antique dealer (an-tique, deal-er): one who sells or buys old out-of-date objects, such as old cars, furniture, and jewelry.

appliance repairman (ap-pli-ance, re-pair-man): one who repairs electrically powered devices for business and household.

appraise (ap-praise): one who estimates the amount, sets prices on land, homes, etc.

archeologist (ar-che-ol-o-gist): one who studies ancient civilization and cultures.

architect (ar-chi-tect): one who design building for construction.

artist (ar-tist): one skilled in craft, drawing and painting.

astrologer (as-trol-o-ger): one who foretells the future.

astronaut (as-tro-naut): one who explores in space.

astronomer (as-tron-o-mer): a expert in astronomy.

assesor (as-ses-or): one who make assessments for taxation.

athlete (ath-lete): one trained in physical exercise and sports.

attorney (at-tor-ney): a lawyer who give advice to clients in court settlements.

Attorney General (at-tor-ney, gen-er-al): the chief law officer of government.

audiologist (audio-lo-gist): one who work with hard of hearing persons.

auctioneer (auc-tion-eer): one who sells properties at an auction to the highest bidder.

auditor (au-di-tor): one who checks and examines personal and business accounts.

auto body specialist (auto-body-spe-cial-ist): one skilled in repairing all kinds of vehicles.

aviator (a-vi-a-tor): a pilot for airplanes, jets, and helicopters.

B

baby-sitter (ba-by-sit-ter): one who takes care of young children while parents are absent.

bacteriologist (bac-te-ri-ol-o-gist): one who studies biology and medicine that deals with bacteria.

bagel shop (ba-gel, shop): a place that sells doughnuts and sweet rolls.

bailsman (bails-man): one who pays debt for a person under arrest.

baker (ba-ker): one who bakes and sells breads, cakes, and pies.

Cakes are just one of many pastry baked at the bakery.

ballerina (bal-le-ri-na): a female ballet dancer.

balloonist (bal-loon-ist): one who travels in a balloon. One who designs inflated balloons for parties and special events.

banker (bank-er): one that engages in the business of *banking.*

barber (bar-ber): one who cuts hair, shaves beards as a business.

barbecue shop (bar-be-cue, shop) : one who sells roasted, or grilled meats
for business.

bargeman (barge-man): one who is in charge of employees in a barge.

barker (bark-er): one who advertises shows at the entrance.

barmaid (bar-maid): a female bartender.

barman (bar-man): a male bartender.

baseball player (base-ball, play-er): one who plays baseball for a living.

Baseball players

basketball player (bas-ket-ball play-er): one who plays basketball in school,
college or NBA.

barroom (bar-room): a room where alcoholic liquids are served.

beautician (beau-ti-cian): one who cuts and styles hair, or gives cosmetic
treatments.

beekeeper (bee-keep-er): one who keeps bees for honey.

bicycle shop (bi-cy-cle, shop): a shop that sells or makes bicycles, its parts, or repairs bicycles.

bicyclist (bi-cy-clist): one who rides a bicycle in races or sports.

billposter (bill-post-er): one who post bills, notices, or advertisements on walls, fences, etc.

binder (bind-er): one who binds books.

biographer (bi-og-ra-pher): one who writes about a person's life.

biologist (bi-ol-o-gist): one who studies the science of life in all its manifestations, organ structure, reproduction growth, and development for living organisms.

bishop (bish-op): the head prelate of the Christian church. The head of a diocese.

blacksmith (black-smith): one who makes shoes for horses.

boatman (boat-man): one who deals with or works on boats.

bodybuilder (body-build-er): one who exercises to increase body strength.

boiler (boil-er): one who is in charge of generating steam for heating power in plants and factories.

bookbinder (book-bind-er): one who trades in binding books.

bodyguard (body-guard): one who is responsible for the safety of others.

bookkeeper (book-keep-er): one who records business transactions.

bookmaker (book-mak-er): one who compiles or binds books.

bookseller (book-sell-er): one who sell books for business.

bouncer (bounc-er): one who is employed to restrain or eject disorderly persons.

boutique (bou-tique): a small fashionable specialty shop or business.

bowler (bowl-er): one who plays bowling.

boxer (box-er): one who engages in the sport of boxing.

brakeman (brake-man): one who tends to brakes on railroad cars or assists in operating trains.

brazier (bra-zier): one who works with brass, elements made of copper and zinc.

bricklayer (brick-lay-er): one who builds with bricks.

bridal shop owner (brid-al, shop, own-er): one who sells wedding attires clothes, flowers, and formal wear.

bridgeworker (bridge-work-er): a person who makes dental bridges for the mouth. One who construct bridges for highways.

broadcaster (broad-cast-er): one who tells the news on radio or television.

broom maker (broom, mak-er): one who makes brooms for sweeping floors.

broncobuster (bron-co-bust-er): one who breaks a bronco to the saddle.

bruiser (bruis-er): a big husky man, or a professional boxer.

brush maker (brush, mak-er): one who makes brushes from animal hair, for dusting, hair, and painting.

bryologist (bry-ol-o-gist): one who studies how to treat mosses.

buckaroo (buck-a-roo): a cowboy.

buffer (buff-er): one who buffs or polishes.

builder (build-er): one that *builds*, especially one that contracts to *build* and supervises *building* operations.

bulldozer operator (bull-doz-er op-er-a-tor): one who operates a bulldozer for moving soil and clearing wooded areas.

Bulldozer operator.

bullfighter (bull-fight-er): one who engages in a public spectacle, performed especially in Spain, Portugal, and parts of Latin America, in which a fighting bull is engaged in a series of traditional maneuver culminating, usually with the ceremonial execution of the bull by sword.

bus driver (bus driv-er): one that drives a bus to carry passengers from place to place.

business owner (busi-ness own-er): one who owns or operates a business, factory, firm, or store.

business man (busi-ness man): one who is engaged in commercial industrial activities.

butcher (butch-er): one who cuts and dresses meats for the markets.

butler (but-ler): the chief male servant of a household who has charge of other employees, receives guests, directs the serving of meals, and performs various personal services.

buyer (buy-er): one who makes purchases for business and stores.

C

cabinet maker (cab-i-net mak-er): one who makes cabinets, furniture, etc.

cable serviceman (ca-ble, ser-vice-man): one who sells or services cable television installation and repairs.

cake decorator (cake, dec-o-ra-tor): one who bakes cakes and decorates with art decorations, as flowers, writings, and pictures for special events.

calligrapher (cal-lig-ra-pher): one who teaches letter designs with beautiful handwriting.

cameraman (cam-era-man): one who operates a camera for television or motion pictures.

campaign manager (cam-paign, man-ag-er): one who directs campaign operations for candidates' party.

camping center (camp-ing, cen-ter): a center or place that sells outdoors shelter, tents, sleeping bags, lanterns, and flashlights for recreation.

candy maker (can-dy mak-er): one who makes candy consisting of sugar syrup, nuts, fruits, or chocolate to eat or sell.

cap shop (cap-shop): one who makes or sell caps or hats to wear.

car dealer (car, deal-er): one who buys, sells, and trades cars.

car painter (car paint-er): one who paints cars.

car washer (car-wash-er): one who operates a place where cars are washed, vacuumed, and waxed.

carpet and rug dealer (car-pet and rug-deal-er): one who is in business to sell carpet, ceramic tile, and floor coverings.

cardiologist (card-i-ol-o-gist): one who specializes with heart problems.

carpenter (car-pen-ter): one who builds or repairs houses and other wooden things.

cartoonist (car-toon-ist): one who does comics strips, drawing or motion pictures.

case worker (case, work-er): one who investigates families that need help with bills, doctors, housing, and money.

cashier (ca-shier): one who collects payments for goods.

cater (ca-ter): one who provides foods and services for social events.

cattle farmer (cat-tle, farm-er): one who raises beef cattle for food and leather.

cattleman (cat-tle-man): one who raises or tends to cattle.

cellular dealer (cel-lu-lar, deal-er): one who sells cellular phone and equipment.

cementer (ce-ment-er): one who pours mixture of clay and limestone for driveways, roads, and streets.

chancellor (chan-cel-lor): the head chief of universities, a judge of a court of *chancery* or equity in various states of the United States.

chandler (chan-dler): one who makes or sells candles.

chauffeur (chau-feur): the automobile driver paid to take passengers from place to place.

chemical plant worker (chem-i-cal, plant work-er): one who works at changing compositions of substances, changing wood to paper, etc.

chemotherapist (che-mo-ther-a-pist): one who gives cancer patients treatments for infections with chemical drugs.

chemist (chem-ist): one trained in chemistry.

chimney sweeper (chim-ney sweep-er): one who cleans soot from the inside of chimneys.

chiropractor (chi-ro-prac-tor): doctors who manipulates body structure.

choreographer (cho-re-og-ra-pher): one who devises ballet and other dance compositions.

circus clown (cir-cus, clown): one who plays jokes, tricks, and entertains in shows and parades.

city manager (city man-ag-er): one who helps manage city affairs.

civil engineer (civ-il, en-gi-neer): a professional engineer who designs, builds bridges and roads as public works.

cleaning worker (clean-ing, work-er): one who cleans homes and offices for business.

clergyman (cler-gy-man): one who preaches God's word.

clerk (clerk): a salesperson in a store or a worker who attends to customers.

clinic worker (clin-ic work-er): one who works at an infirmary or medical building that treats patients. A place for laboratory experimenting.

clothing buyer (cloth-ing, buy-er): one who purchases clothes to sell.

clothing factor (cloth-ing, fac-tor): a business where clothes are made to sell to stores.

coach (coach): a trainer or tutor for sports and athletic events.

coal miner (coal min-er): one who works in coal mines.

columnist (col-um-nist): one who writes special stories for books and newspapers.

comedian (co-me-di-an): one who writes and tells funny jokes.

commentator (com-men-ta-tor): one who writes and discusses news events.

communication engineer (com-mu-ni-ca-tion, en-gi-neer): one who deals with transmitting messages between places and persons, in the telephone system, control system, and digital control.

composer (com-pos-er): one who writes music and songs.

computer engineer (com-put-er, en-gi-neer): one who specializes in electronic machine memory system of high speed and development.

computer technician (com-put-er, tech-ni-cian): one who specializes in operation and performance of computers.

congressman (con-gress-man): a member of the U.S. House of Representatives or Congress.

conservationist (con-ser-va-tion-ist): one who keeps preservation of natural resources, as forests, fish, and wildlife.

consultant (con-sul-tant): one who gives advice on business affairs.

cook (cook): one who prepares food for eating.

cookie maker (cook-ie, mak-er): one who bakes and prepares small thin cakes to eat or sell.

coordinator (co-or-di-na-tor): one who ranks, puts in order, files, and fixes elements.

copyboy (copy-boy): an errand boy in a newspaper office.

copyist (copy-ist): one who makes copies or documents.

copyreader (copy-read-er): one who edits work intended for publication.

copywriter (copy-writ-er): one who writes copy for advertisements.

coroner (cor-o-ner): one who investigates causes of deaths.

corpsman (corps-man): one who enlisted in the U.S. Army as a pharmacist or hospital assistant.

cosmetic salesperson (cos-met-ic, sales-per-son): one who sells cosmetic products for complexion, body, and hands.

cotton farmer (cot-ton, farm-er): a farmer who raises cotton for cloth and fabric etc.

cowboy (cow-boy): one who works on a ranch tending to cattles.

craftsman (crafts-man): one who is skilled in craft and art.

criminologist (crim-i-nol-o-gist): one who studies and investigates crime and behavior of criminals and misbehaving persons.

D

dairy farmer (dairy farm-er): one who raises cows for milk, cheese, and butter.

dancer (danc-er): one who performs steps, such as with waltz and the tango with music.

day care person (day, care, per-son): one who operates a center that keeps children under school age.

day laborer (day la-bor-er): one who works for daily wages especially as an unskilled laborer.

dean (dean): the head of a division, faculty, college, or school of a university.

detective (de-tec-tive): one who investigates crimes and discovers evidence.

deep sea diver (deep, sea, div-er): one who explores, investigates, and studies plants and animals in deep water.

delivery person (de-liv-ery, per-son): one who delivers or distributes goods and merchandises, etc.

dental assistant (den-tal, as-sis-tant): one who helps the dentist.

dentist (den-tist): one who diagnoses and treats diseases of teeth.

dermatologist (der-ma-tol-o-gist): one who is trained in medical science to treat skin diseases.

diamond cutter (di-a-mond, cut-ter): one who cuts and shapes diamonds in various forms.

die maker (die, mak-er): one who gives metal tools various shapes by molding under pressure.

dietitian (di-e-ti-tian): a skilled person who regulates diets.

diplomatist (di-plo-ma-tist): one who is skillful in dealing with foreign affairs.

director (di-rec-tor): one who is in charge of activities, programs directors of parks and tours.

dishwasher (dish-wash-er): one who washes dishes for a job.

disk jockey (disk, jock-ey): an announcer and commentator for radio programs.

dispatcher (dis-patch-er): one who sends out airlines, buses, trains, taxicabs on schedule.

diver (div-er): one who dives in water to salvage sunken cargo or recover drowned victims.

doctor (doc-tor): a person who has earned one of the highest academic degrees (as a PhD) conferred by a university. One skilled or specializing in healing arts, especially a physician, surgeon, dentist, or veterinarian who is licensed to practice.

dog catcher (dog, catch-er): one who impounds (catches) stray dogs.

dog trainer (dog, train-er): one who trains dogs to be obedient or to perform tricks.

doorman (door-man): an attendant who assists persons entering and leaving buildings.

doughnut shop (dough-nut shop): one who sells doughnuts and other pastries.

draftsman (drafts-man): one who draws designs and plans homes and buildings.

drapery dealer (drap-ery deal-er): a dealer of cloth for window curtains and fashion.

dressmaker (dress-mak-er): one who makes dresses or women's clothes.

drillmaster (drill-mas-ter): one who teaches or trains persons for drills and exercises. The captain of the drill team.

drummer (drum-mer): one who plays the drum.

E

ecologist (ecol-o-gist): one who studies all living thing environments, water, earth, and air.

economist (econ-o-mist): a specialist in *economics.*

editor (ed-i-tor): someone who *edits* especially as an occupation.

electrician (elec-tri-cian): one who installs and repairs electrical equipment.

electronics engineering (elec-tron-ics, en-gi-neer-ing): one who designs or works with electronic devices.

embroider (em-broi-der): one who designs in needlework. One who sews ornaments on clothes with designs.

embryologist (em-bry-ol-o-gist): one who studies the development of embryos.

encyclopedist (en-cy-clo-pe-dist): one who compiles or writes for an *encyclopedia.*

endocrinologist (en-do-cri-nol-o-gist): one who studies and works in the medical field dealing with endocrine glands.

engineer (en-gi-neer): a designer or builder of *engines.*

engraver (en-grav-er): one who carves figures and letters into metal, stone, or wood.

entertainer (en-ter-tain-er): one who entertains guests by performing on stage, singing, etc.

estimator (es-ti-ma-tor): one who forms opinion about time, amount, and costs for services.

essayist (es-say-ist): a writer of essays, term paper, or speech.

esthete (es-thete): one who is keen in beauty and art.

ethnologist (eth-nol-o-gist): one who studies racial and ethnic groups and their origins.

evangelist (evan-gel-ist): one who preaches the Gospel by spreading the good news.

examiner (ex-am-in-er): one who tests for knowledge, inspects and asks questions.

executioner (ex-e-cu-tion-er): one who executes death sentence.

executive (ex-ec-u-tive): one who manages the administrative affairs of business.

expert (ex-pert): one who has special skills and training as a specialist.

experimenter (ex-per-i-ment-er): one who tests for truth, facts, and knowledge based on results from experimenting.

explorer (ex-plor-er): one who travels, searches, and examines to find knowledge.

exterminator (ex-ter-mi-na-tor): one who helps to control pests, bugs, insects, and termites in buildings.

F

fabric center (fab-ric cen-ter): a place where sewing materials are sold.

factory worker (fac-to-ry work-er): one who does manual labor where goods are manufactured.

farmer (farm-er): a person who cultivates land, crops or raises animals or fish.

fashion designer (fash-ion de-sign-er): one who designs clothes for fashion.

fast-food restaurant (fast-food, res-tau-rant): a place where foods are provided fast: hamburgers and other sandwiches, soft drinks and ice creams.

fencer (fenc-er): one who encloses an area with rails, stakes, wire, wood, iron, and bricks.

fertilizer retailer (fer-til-iz-er, re-tail-er): one who sells fertilizers.

figure skater (fig-ure, skat-er): one who skates and dances in harmonious patterns.

film developer (film, de-vel-op-er): one who develops films from cameras.

film maker (film mak-er): one who direct for filming shows and motion pictures.

finisher (fin-ish-er): one who gives furniture a glossy finish with paint or polish.

fireman (fire-man): one who prevents fires. One who rescues people from burning buildings and accidents.

fireplace system (fire-place, sys-tem): one who makes or builds fire place equipments to sell.

fisherman (fish-er-man): one who fishes for a career or for sport.

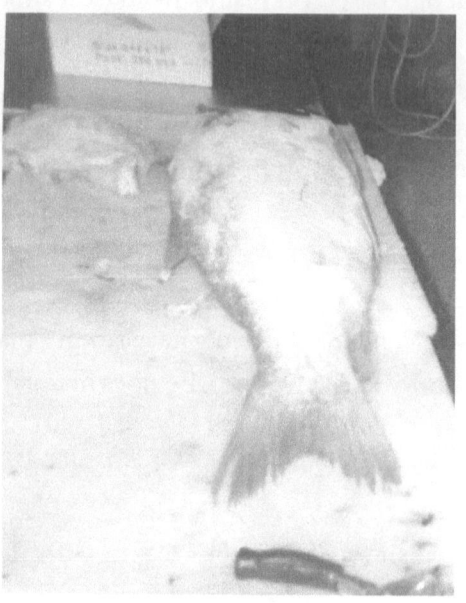

What would a fisherman want to catch?

fishmonger (fish-mong-er): one who deals with hatching fish for commercial use.

fitness center (fit-ness, cen-ter): a business equipped for exercise and workout activities.

flagman (flag-man): one who signals with flags for street crossings and rail road crossings.

flight attendant (flight, at-ten-dant): one who attends to passengers on airplanes.

flight engineer (flight, en-gi-neer): one who is in charge of mechanical operation during flight.

florist (flo-rist): one who arranges and sells flowers.

food worker (food work-er): one who prepares foods for business.

football player (foot-ball, play-er): one who plays football on a team.

foreman (fore-man): one who oversees groups of workers.

forester (for-est-er): one who is skilled in forestry or in charge of a forest.

The forester works in the forest.

fortune teller (for-tune tell-er): one who tells the future or make predictions of one's life.

formal wear shop (for-mal, wear-shop): a shop that rents or sells elaborate. dress for special occasion, as evening attire, gowns, tuxedos, etc.

furrier (fur-ri-er): one who deals with fur and fur garments.

G

gallery (gal-lery): a room or shop where statures, paintings, flowers, etc. are on display or are sold.

gambler (gam-bler): one who bets, and takes chances on something of value.

game keeper (game, keep-er): one who takes care of games. One in charge of game activities.

game maker (game, mak-er): one who makes games for play activities, contests, for winning or profession, business, and teaching.

garbage collector (gar-bage col-lec-tor): one who collects waste and refuse.

gardener (gar-den-er): one who plants flowers and vegetables to grow in a small area.

Gardener works with flowers and plants.

garment factory worker (gar-ment, fac-to-ry, work-er): one who works at the factory that makes clothing.

gas station owner (gas sta-tion, own-er): one who supplies gasoline and oil to motor vehicles.

gasman (gasman): one who reads gas meters for the amount of gas used by business, homes, and schools.

gemologist (gem-ol-o-gist): one who is trained and has a certificate in identifying diamonds and gemstones.

general officer (gen-er-al, of-fi-cer): the highest rank in the U.S. Army.

genetic engineer (ge-net-ic, en-gi-neer): one who studies science dealing with interaction of genes in producing and developing organisms.

geodesist (ge-od-e-sist): one who specializes in dealing with the earth, mapping, continents, and locating special points.

geographer (ge-og-ra-pher): one who deals with describing the surface of the earth and its characteristics.

geologist (ge-ol-o-gist): one who studies the origin and structure of the the earth.

geological engineering (ge-o-log-ical en-gi-neer-ing): one who deals with mineral deposits and operations.

geometrician (geo-me-tri-cian): a specialist in geometry; one that knows mathematics that deals with space, lines, points, numbers, etc.

gerontologist (ger-on-tol-o-gist): one who studies the process of aging.

glass blower (glass, blow-er): one who blows steam or air through a tube to mold glass in various shapes.

goat farmer (goat, farm-er): one who raises goats for milk and cheese.

golfer (golf-er): one who plays golf.

goldsmith (gold-smith): one who deals with articles of gold.

goodwill store (goodwill-store): a store that provides goods for charity.

governor (gov-er-nor): one who governs the state, the chief of any state government.

grader (grad-er): one who grades or inspects goods.

grain farmer (grain-farm-er): one who raises or grows corn, rice, oats, and wheat.

graphologist (gra-phol-o-gist): one who studies handwriting.

grave digger (grave, dig-ger): one who digs graves to bury the dead.

gravestone maker (grave-stone, mak-er): one who makes stone markers for graves.

greeting card shop (greet-ing, card shop): a shop where cards are sold that congratulates, greets, salutes, and welcomes.

guitarist (gui-tar-ist): one who plays a guitar.

gunner (gun-ner): one who operates a gun.

gun shop (gun-shop): a place where guns are sold or traded.

gunsmith (gun-smith): one who makes or repairs guns.

gymnast (gym-nast): one who is skilled in gymnastics.

gynecologist (gy-ne-col-o-gist): one who specializes in a branch of medicine that deals with diseases, and routine physical care of the reproductive system of women.

H

hair products business (hair, prod-ucts, business): a business selling hair products and treatments, selling shampoo, conditioner, etc.

hairstylist (hair-styl-ist): one who styles, cuts, and arranges hairstyles.

handyman (handy-man): one who performs odd jobs.

hardware store (hard-ware, store): one who sells metal tools, utensils, and machinery.

harvest man (ha-vest, man): one who labors at gathering ripened fruits, nuts and vegetables on farms and orchards.

heating and air condition business (heat-ing and air con-di-tion busi-ness): a business to install air conditioning and heating units.

heavy equipment operator (heavy, e-quip-ment, op-er-a-tor): a business that works with moving heavy weight, rocks, irons, soil, etc.

helicopter pilot (he-li-cop-ter, pi-lot): one who operates a helicopter.

herpetologist (her-pe-tol-o-gist): one who treats reptiles and amphibians.

highway patrols (high-way, pa-trols): a police officer who patrols the highways for protection. One who checks for speeding and dishonesty on streets and roads.

hockey player (hock-ey, play-er): one who plays a game wearing ice skates and helmet; the player drives a disk into the opponent's goal.

hog farmer (hog, farm-er): one who raises hogs for the market or for food.

home economist (home, econ-o-mist): one who practices homemaking.

homemaker (home-mak-er): one in charge of managing the home; as a housewife.

hospital worker (hos-pi-tal, work-er): one who works in a hospital that provides medical treatments, patient assistance, or house cleaning.

horseman (hor-se-man): a man who is skilled in managing horses.

horsewoman (horse-wom-an): a woman who is skilled in managing horses.

horticulturist (hor-ti-cul-tur-ist): one who studies how to grow garden vegetables, fruits and flowers, etc.

hotel manager (ho-tel man-ag-er): one who manages hotels that provides lodging to travelers.

housekeeper (house-keep-er): one who is paid to do housework service in homes and businesses.

housemaster (house-mas-ter): one who is in charge of homes for boys and girls at school, college, or resort.

humanitarian (hu-man-i-tar-i-an): one who seeks to promote the welfare of mankind.

hunter (hunt-er): one who hunts game.

hydrologist (hy-drol-o-gist): one who deals with water, earth, their characteristics and effects in relation to human activities.

hygienist (hy-gien-ist): one who studies the principles of health science.

I

ice-cream shop (ice-cream, shop): a shop, a stand, or truck that sells or makes ice cream.

ice hockey player (ice-hockey, play-er): one who plays a hockey game on ice.

ice-skater (ice-skat-er): one who dances, glides, or moves on ice, wearing ice skates.

iceman (ice-man): one who supplies or delivers ice to consumers.

ichthyologist (ich-thy-ol-o-gist): one who studies zoology and treats fish.

ideologist (ide-ol-o-gist): one who formulates vision and speculation.

illustrator (il-lus-tra-tor): one who explains, shows, to make clear his illustration; one who draws pictures for books.

industrial engineer (in-dus-tri-al, en-gi-neer): someone who deals with the design, improvement, and installation of integrated systems as of people, materials, and energy in industry.

industry worker (in-dus-try work-er): one who works in manufacturing goods.

inquisitor (in-quis-i-tor): one who inquires, investigates, or examines.

inspector (in-spec-tor): one who looks, checks, examines goods and products carefully before packing and shipping.

instructor (in-struc-tor): one who teaches class lessons.

Instructor. Teacher in charge of a class.

instrumentalist (in-stru-men-tal-ist): one who plays a musical instrument.

insulator (in-su-la-tor): one who uses materials to insulate homes and buildings.

insurance salesman (in-sur-ance, sales-man): one who sells insurance for loss and damage in accidents, death, fire, health, homes, and businesses.

interior decorator (in-te-ri-or, dec-o-ra-tor): one who decorates furnishings with beautiful arrangements for business offices and homes.

internist (in-ter-nist): a specialist in internal medicine.

interpreter (in-ter-pret-er): one who translates language for people speaking different languages.

inventor (in-ven-tor): one who invents, creates, or makes some kind of device.

ironer (iron-er): one who irons clothes for business.

J

jailer (jail-er): one in charge of putting persons in jail, awaiting trial.

janitor (jan-i-tor): one who keeps floors and buildings free of trash and debris.

jeweller (jew-el-ler): one who makes jewelry, or a dealer who sells jewelry.

jobber (job-ber): one who buys goods in bulk quantities from manufacturers and sell them to the retailers.

jockey (jock-ey): a horseback racer.

juggler (jug-gler): one skilled in keeping several objects in motion in the air at the same time by alternately tossing and catching them.

joker (jok-er): one who tells jokes.

journalist (jour-nal-ist): one who writes, edits and publishes newspapers.

judge (judge): one who hears cases in court and makes decisions on who are guilty or not guilty.

judicator (ju-di-ca-tor): one who acts as a judge.

junk man (junk-man): one who collects junk, scraps, or trash to sell or keep.

jurist (ju-rist): one skilled in law.

juryman (ju-ry-man): one who serves on juror duty; one who makes decisions or verdicts.

justice of peace (jus-tice of peace): one who has authority to fine and imprison in minor case.

juvenile officer (ju-ve-nile of-fi-cer): an officer elected to direct neglected, and delinquent children, involved with violation of the law; one who counsels young persons with punishment and criminal cases.

K

karate teacher (ka-ra-te, teach-er): one who teaches karate, an oriental method of hand to hand combat using sudden forceful blows with side of the hand.

keeper (keep-er): one who keeps guard or takes care of young people, and the sick.

kennel owner (ken-nel, own-er): one who houses dogs to breed and train to sell.

key maker (key, mak-er): one who makes instruments for moving bolts, or locks.

kindergarten teacher (kin-der-gar-ten, teach-er): one who teaches a class of young children age four to six.

L

lab technician (lab tech-ni-cian): one who is trained for special work in space or the medical field.

landscape architect (land-scape, ar-chi-tect): one who plans and arrange outdoor features, plants and trees, etc.

landholder (land-hold-er): one who owns land.

landlady (land-la-dy): a woman who rents apartments, rooms, and homes.

lapidary (lap-i-dary): one who cuts, engraves, and polishes stone.

Latinist (Lat-in-ist): a specialist in the Latin language or Roman culture.

laundryman (laun-dry-man): a man that manages a commercial laundry.

laundry woman (laun-dry, wom-an): a woman that manages a commercial laundry.

lawn mower dealer (lawn-mow-er, deal-er): one who sells lawn mowers and parts.

lawmaker (law-mak-er): one who enacts laws.

lawyer (law-yer): one who advises clients and represents clients in courts.

lender (lend-er): one who lends money and grants loans.

librarian (li-brar-i-an): one who has charge of a library where books are kept.

lieutenant (lieu-ten-ant): a commissioned officer holding either of two ranks, first or second lieutenant.

lieutenant governor (lieu-ten-ant gov-er-nor): an elected officer who performs duties in the absence of the governor.

lifeguard (life-guard): an expert swimmer employed to protect safety of swimmers at beaches, pools, and swimming areas.

light fixtures shop (light, fix-tures, shop): a shop that sells light fixtures, for homes, businesses, streets, and yards.

limousine serviceman (lim-ou-sine, ser-vice-man): one who operates luxurious large automobiles for passengers to ride.

lineman (line-man): a man who installs or repairs telephone or electric power lines.

linguist (lin-guist): one who is fluent in several languages.

liquor salesperson (li-quor, sales-per-son): one who sells alcoholic beverage, beer, brandy, whisky, and wine.

locksmith (lock-smith): one who unlocks doors and makes and repairs locks.

locomotive engineer (lo-co-mo-tive, en-gi-neer): one who works with freight trains to move from place to place.

logger (log-ger): one who works with cutting, loading, and hauling logs.

Where would loggers work?

long-shore-man (long-shore-man): one who works on waterfront to load and unload vessels.

lumber man (lum-ber-man): one who sells lumber used for building homes, etc.

lutanist (lu-ta-nist): one who plays a lute.

lyricist (lyr-i-cist): one who writes words to songs for music.

M

machinist (ma-chin-ist): one who is skilled in operation or repair of machines.

magician (ma-gi-cian): one who performs magic and tricks of illusion.

maidservant (maid-ser-vant): a person hired to assist in domestic services.

mailman (mail-man): one who carries and delivers mail.

maintenance worker (main-te-nance, work-er): one who keeps roads, machines, and buildings in good condition.

The mailman delivers the mail daily.

makeup artist (make-up, art-ist): one who makes a person look as glamorous as possible; one who changes a person's appearance.

manager (man-ag-er): one who manages or directs business; the hotel or store manager.

manicurist (man-i-cur-ist): one who cuts, trims, polishes, and massages hands and feet for health and beauty.

marine engineer (ma-rine en-gi-neer): one who specializes in mechanical engineering and operations of ships and cost of fuel.

mariner (mar-i-ner): one who assists in navigating ships and sailors or seamen.

marketer (mar-ket-er): one seeking to buy, sell, or trade a specific service or commodity.

matchmaker (match-mak-er): one who brings about marriage between two persons; one who arranges an athletic match; one who makes matches for lighting fires.

mathematician (math-e-ma-ti-cian): one who is an expert in solving math problems.

mayor (may-or): the chief officer of a city.

mechanic (me-chan-ic): one who makes and repairs machines and tools.

merchant (mer-chant): one who buys and sells commodities for a profit.

messenger (mes-sen-ger): one who works in running errands or sending messages.

metallurgist (met-al-lur-gist): one who changes metals to ores or one who works with metals.

meteorologist (me-te-o-rol-o-gist): one who tells weather conditions.

midwife (mid-wife): a woman who assists women in childbirth.

military engineer (mil-i-tary en-gi-neer): one who deals with military purposes, warfare, field engineering and armed forces.

military police (mil-i-tary po-lice): soldiers who perform police duty.

milkmaid (milk-maid): a woman who milks cows or works in a dairy.

milkman (milk-man): a man who sells or delivers milk.

miller (mill-er): one who operates or tends to mills.

milliner (mil-li-ner): one who makes or sells women's hats.

millionaire (mil-lion-aire): one whose wealth is valued at a million.

millwright (mill-wright): one who plans, builds, or repairs mills.

miner (min-er): one who works in a mine; one who digs the earth to obtain coal, stone or ore.

minister (min-is-ter): a church clergyman.

missionary (mis-sion-ary): one who is sent out to educate others on religious doctrine in foreign countries.

model (mod-el): one who poses, wearing clothes for fashion to be displayed in magazines, etc.

moonshiner (moon-shin-er): a maker or seller of illicit whiskey.

mopper (mop-per): one who mops floors.

monument dealer (mon-u-ment, deal-er): one who makes or sells tombstone markers, for cemeteries in memory of the deceased.

moralist (mor-al-ist): a teacher of morals.

mortician (mor-ti-cian): one who prepares the deceased for the final resting place.

motorcycle dealer (mo-tor-cy-cle, deal-er): one who sells motorcycles, water vehicles, and accessories.

motorman (mo-tor-man): one who operates electric street cars.

mountaineer (moun-tain-eer): one who climbs mountains.

mover (mov-er): one who moves household goods for a business.

movie theater operator (mov-ie, the-ater, op-er-a-tor): one in charged of operating a building to present motion pictures.

movie star (mov-ie, star): a film actor who plays in motion pictures and theaters.

multimillionaire (mul-ti-mil-lion-aire): one having a fortune of many millions of dollars.

muffler shop owner (muf-fler, shop, own-er): one who replaces mufflers on vehicles to reduce noise.

musician (mu-si-cian): one who is skilled in playing a musical instrument.

Judy is a musician.

music mart (mu-sic, mart): a place that sells musical instruments, stereo sounds, sound speakers, CDs, records, and tapes.

musicologist (mu-si-col-o-gist): one who studies *music* as a branch of knowledge or field of research as distinct from composition or performance.

mythologist (my-thol-o-gist): one who studies imaginary, fictitious events and people.

N

naturalist (nat-u-ral-ist): one who is versed in natural history.

navigator (nav-i-ga-tor): one who is trained to steer aircraft, missiles, and ships.

newsstand (news-stand): a place that sells newspapers to the public.

newsboy (news-boy): one who delivers newspapers.

news reporter (news, re-port-er): one who reports the news on radio or television.

news printer (news, print-er): one who prints the newspaper for selling.

neurologist (neu-rol-o-gist): one who is trained to deal with people with nervous disorders.

novelist (nov-el-ist): one who writes books.

nurse (nurse): one who is trained to care for the sick.

nursery (nurs-ery): an area where plants are grown for transplanting, for budding and grafting, or for sale. A room for small children.

nursery teacher (nurs-ery, teach-er): one who trains children under four before entering kindergarten.

nursing home worker (nurs-ing, home, work-er): one who takes care of persons unable to care for themselves.

nutritionist (nu-tri-tion-ist): a specialist who promotes good nutritious foods for growth and development.

O

obstetrician (ob-ste-tri-cian): a specialist dealing with childbirth and pregnancy.

occupational therapist (oc-cu-pa-tion-al, ther-a-pist): someone who administers therapy based on engagement in meaningful activities of daily life (as self-care skills, education, work, or social interaction) especially to enable or encourage participation in such activities despite impairments or limitations in physical or mental functioning.

oilman (oil-man): one who studies oil fields and oil wells and drills to find crude oil and petroleum.

opthalmologist (oph-thal-mol-o-gist): a specialist who deals with structure, functions, and diseases of the eye.

optician (op-ti-cian): one who deals with improving eyesight.

optometrist (op-tom-e-trist): a specialist who measures vision and prescribes corrective lenses for visual defects.

orchard grower (or-chard, grow-er): one who has a plantation that grows fruits, nuts, and trees.

organist (or-gan-ist): one who plays the organ.

orthodontist (or-tho-don-tist): a specialist who deals with correcting and prevention of irregularities of the teeth.

ornithologist (or-ni-thol-o-gist): one who studies how to treat birds.

orthographist (or-thog-ra-phist): one who studies how to spell words correctly.

osteologist (os-te-ol-o-gist): one who studies structure of bones and skeletons.

otologist (o-tol-o-gist): physician who specializes with the ear and its diseases.

P

painter (paint-er): one who covers surfaces with a coat of paint.

paleontologist (pa-le-on-tol-o-gist): a scientist who studies fossils and dinosaurs; one who studies the bodies of dinosaurs.

palmist (palm-ist): one who practices discovering persons' future from reading lines and marks in the palms of the hands.

paper hanger (pa-per, hang-er): one who covers walls with paper for business.

paper plant worker (pa-per, plant, work-er): one whose work involves making paper from pulpwood to form thin sheets for writing, tissue, bags, and towels.

paramedics (par-a-med-ic): a trained medical worker, who gives emergency care, chiefly to accident victims or to persons with sudden illnesses.

park director (park, di-rec-tor): one who manages places for public use and pleasure.

parole officer (pa-role, of-fi-cer): one who is in charge of releasing prisoners before the sentence expires.

pathologist (pa-thol-o-gist): one who is skilled in medical science, who diagnoses the origin and nature of diseases.

patternmaker (pat-tern-mak-er): one who makes models or guides for making craft and clothes.

pawnbroker (pawn-bro-ker): one who lends money at interest on personal property.

pediatrician (pe-di-a-tri-cian): a physician who specializes in diseases and treatment of children.

perfumer (per-fum-er): one who makes or sells perfumes and fragrance for the body.

pet groomer (pet, groom-er): one who grooms pets by bathing and trimming pets' fur.

pet shop owner (pet, shop, own-er): one who sells tamed animals for pets.

petrologist (pe-trol-o-gist): one who studies the characteristics of rocks.

pharmacist (phar-ma-cist): a person licensed to engage in pharmacy.

photographer (pho-tog-ra-pher): one who takes pictures and slides with a camera.

What does the photographer use?

physical therapist (phys-i-cal, ther-a-pist): someone who administers the treatment of disease by physical and mechanical means, as massage, regulated exercise, water, light, heat, and electricity.

physician (phy-si-cian): a doctor that is licensed to practice medicine.

physicist (phys-i-cist): a specialist in physics, the science that deals with energy, matter, and motion.

pianist (pi-a-nist): a piano player.

pilot (pi-lot): one who operates an aircraft during flights.

piper (pip-er): one who installs pipe lines.

pitcher (pitch-er): one who throws the ball for baseball games.

pitchman (pitch-man): one who sells small articles from stands or side walk as venders.

pitman (pit-man): a worker in a mine.

plant manager (plant, man-ag-er): one who oversees business at chemical plants, enterprises, and manufacturing plants.

plastic surgeon (plas-tic, sur-geon): one who restores deformed body parts.

plumber (plumb-er): one who installs and repairs pipes for businesses and homes.

poet (po-et): one who writes poems.

police (police): an officer who protects and maintains order in cities and towns.

political economist (po-lit-i-cal, econ-o-mist): a person skilled in economy, management of wealth, financial matters, and resources of a country.

politician (pol-i-ti-cian): one who is engaged in government affairs.

porter (por-ter): one who carries travelers' luggage at airports and buses; a keeper at doors and gates in hotels.

postman (post-man): a mailman; one who delivers the mail.

postmaster (post-mas-ter): one in charge of the post office.

postmaster general (post-master, gen-er-al): the executive head of the post office.

potato grower (po-ta-to grow-er): one who grows potatoes.

potter (pot-ter): one who makes earthenware or vessels foam clay.

poultry farmer (poul-try farm-er): one who raises chickens, etc.

practical nurse (prac-ti-cal nurse): one who has training in nursing but is not a registered nurse.

preacher (preach-er): one who preaches God's word.

precentor (pre-cen-tor): one who leads the singing of church choir or congregation.

preceptor (pre-cep-tor): a teacher or instructor.

president (pres-i-dent): one who presides over a company, college, or government body.

press agent (press, agent): one is who employed to advance the interests of actors, singers, etc.

pressman (press-man): a man in charge of printing news, as a journalist.

priest (priest): a clergyman ranking over the Roman Catholic Church.

primatologist (pri-ma-tol-o-gist): one who deals with origin, structure, evolution, and classification of primates.

prime minister (prime min-is-ter): the chief official of a cabinet or government.

prince (prince): a male member or a royal family.

princess (prin-cess): a female member of a royal family.

principal (prin-ci-pal): the head of a school under the superintendent.

private detective (pri-vate, de-tec-tive): a policeman who investigates crimes, and unlawful conducts.

probation officer (pro-ba-tion of-fi-cer): one who supervises offenders on suspended sentence.

producer (pro-duc-er): one who produces movies and plays.

professor (pro-fes-sor): a teacher at a university, college, or sometimes secondary school.

professional athlete (pro-fes-sion-al, ath-lete): a skillful athlete that is paid to compete in sport.

projectionist (pro-jec-tion-ist): one who shows motion picture slides on a screen.

promoter (pro-mot-er): one that *promotes, especially* one who assumes the financial responsibilities of a sporting event (as a boxing match) including contracts with the principals, renting the site, and collecting gate receipts.

prophet (proph-et): A religious leader.

proofreader (proof-read-er): one who corrects essays, writings, and printed materials.

Professional athletics are skillful in sports.

prospector (pros-pec-tor): one who searches or examines for minerals.

prosecuting attorney (pros-e-cut-ing, at-tor-ney): an attorney for the state who carries out legal proceedings for criminal suits.

prosthodontist (pros-tho-don-tist): one who makes crowns, bridges, dentures, and artificial teeth.

psychiatrist (psy-chi-a-trist): a physician specializing on mental disorder treatment.

psychologist (psy-chol-o-gist): one who studies the human mind and the behavior of the individual.

psychotherapist (psy-cho-ther-a-pist): one who treats mental or emotional disorder related by *psychological* means.

pulpwood worker (pulp-wood, work-er): one who cuts and hauls logs to the mill for making wood and paper products.

pumpkin grower (pump-kin, grow-er): a farmer that grows pumpkins.

Kindergarten having fun in a pumpkin patch.

public utility worker (pub-lic, util-i-ty, work-er): one who works for the public, supplying electricity, gas, water, etc. under city or state regulations.

public relations worker (pub-lic, re-la-tions, work-er): one who promotes advertising in business with marking activities and press contact.

publisher (pub-lish-er): one in business to publish books and newspapers.

puppeteer (pup-pe-teer): one who manipulates puppets.

printer (print-er): one who reproduces designs, letters, numbers, and pictures on another surface.

Q

queen (queen): the wife of a king; a female chosen in beauty pageants.

quilt maker (quilt, mak-er): one who makes bedcovers to give warmth or for ornamental purposes.

R

racer (rac-er): anyone who races in sports and in tracks.

race car driver (race, car, driv-er): one who drives a high-speed race car.

radio announcer (ra-dio, an-nounc-er): one who talks on the radio in broadcasting programs.

radiologist (ra-di-ol-o-gist): a physician specializing in the medical radiology.

rancher (ranch-er): one who manages a farm raising cattle, horses, and sheep.

rap singer (rap, sing-er): one who sings with rapid repetition in rhyme and slang music.

reader (read-er): one who reads manuscripts for corrections.

real estate consultants (re-al, es-tate, con-sul-tants): one who gives advice, appraising on homes and lands before making a purchase.

receptionist (re-cep-tion-ist): one who receives telephone calls, meets guests at the entrance in offices.

recorder (re-cord-er): one who records written accounts, documents, and other events.

referee (ref-er-ee): a sports official usually having final authority in administering games.

registered nurse (reg-is-tered nurse): a licensed nurse of the state.

rehabilitation counselor (re-ha-bil-i-ta-tion, coun-sel-or): one who gives advice, therapy, and training to restore an ill person to good health.

repairman (re-pair-man): one who repairs things that need restoring; TV or machine repairman.

researcher (re-search-er): one who investigates, studies, and inquires for information.

restaurateur (res-tau-ra-teur): one who operates a restaurant.

rhymester (rhyme-ster): one who makes rapid repetition in rhymes.

ringmaster (ring-mas-ter): the head of a circus ring and performance.

rocketeer (rock-e-teer): a scientist who specializes in *rockets*.

roofer (roof-er): one who covers roofs on homes and buildings.

ropewalker (rope-walk-er): one who walks on a tightrope for circus shows.

roughrider (rough-ri-der): one skilled in breaking broncos, performing dangerous acts in horsemanship.

ruler (rul-er): one who rules or governs. A decision maker.

runner (run-ner): one who runs in races such as a track runner.

S

sacker (sack-er): one who bags goods and merchandise for customers.

safety engineer (safe-ty, en-gi-neer): one who develops methods and procedures to safeguard workers from hazardous work.

salesgirl (sales-girl): a female worker hired to sell merchandise in stores.

sales representative (sales, rep-re-sen-ta-tive): one who represents his business or company by selling their goods.

sampler (sam-pler): one that collects, prepares, or examines *samples*.

sanitation man (san-i-ta-tion, man): one who collects trash and wastes.

satellite dealer (sat-el-lite, deal-er): one who makes or sells satellite systems.

sausage maker (sau-sage, mak-er): one who makes and sells sausages.

sawmill worker (saw-mill, work-er): one who works at mills sawing logs.

sawyer (saw-yer): one who saws logs and wood into lumber.

scenarist (sce-nar-ist): a writer of scenarios.

scholar (schol-ar): one who has high esteem for learning, research, and writing on special topics.

scientist (sci-en-tist): one who studies and discovers with highly specialized scientific skills.

sculptor (sculp-tor): one who carves clay, plastic, or wood into figure statues.

secret service agent (se-cret, ser-vice, agent): one who investigates, undercover about persons or businesses.

seaman (sea-man): one who is in charge of handling boats and ships.

seamstress (seam-stress): one who is skilled in sewing and needlework.

secretary (sec-re-tary): one employed to handle correspondence, manage routine and detail work for a supervisor.

security contractor (se-cu-ri-ty, con-trac-tor): one who supplies security for businesses, persons, or properties.

seedsman (seeds-man): one who sells seeds.

seismologist (seis-mol-o-gist): one who studies earthquakes.

seller (sell-er): one who sells merchandise for business.

sewer worker (sew-er, work-er): one who clean pipes draining and waste materials.

sexologist (sex-ol-o-gist): one who deals with human sexual behavior.

sharecropper (share-crop-per): a tenant farmer who pays a share of his crop as rent for his land.

shepherd (shep-herd): one who watches or guides sheep.

sheriff (sher-iff): the chief officer of counties to enforce law and order.

shipbuilder (ship-build-er): one who builds ships and vessels.

shirt shop (shirt shop): a shop that designs T-shirts with monograms. A shop that sells shirts.

shoemaker (shoe-mak-er): one who makes or repairs shoes.

shoe shiner (shoe shin-er): one who shines, polishes, and waxes shoes for business.

shopkeeper (shop-keep-er): one who operates a shop or store for business.

shore patrol officer (shore, pa-trol, of-fi-cer): one who patrols beaches as coast guards for safety.

showman (show-man): the producer of plays or shows. One who shows merchandise to buyers.

siding maker (sid-ing, mak-er): one who makes and sells boarding that covers homes.

sign maker (sign, mak-er): one who makes signs to announce business events.

sign language expert (sign, lan-guage, ex-pert): one who uses hand gestures for persons incapable of hearing.

singer (sing-er): one who sings as a profession or for entertainment.

sitter (sit-ter): one who sits and takes care of small children, elder and ill persons.

skin diver (skin, div-er): an underwater swimmer or explorer.

skinner (skin-ner): one who sells animals' skins for bags, belts, and shoes.

skipper (skip-per): the captain of a ship.

sky diver (sky, div-er): one who jumps from airplanes with a parachute, performing for entertainment.

skywriter (sky-writ-er): one who forms words in the sky from the vapor of airplanes.

snake charmer (snake, charm-er): entertainer who exhibits power to charm snakes.

soap maker (soap, mak-er): one who makes and sells soap and detergent.

soap opera actor(soap, op-era, ac-tor): one who does drama acting on television.

social worker (so-cial, work-er): any clinical service provider that gives aid to the elder, young, and to needy families.

sociologist (so-ci-ol-o-gist): one who studies evolution of human society

soft drink maker (soft, drink, mak-er): one who makes and sells nonalcoholic drinks.

soldier (sol-dier): one who serves in the United States 'or others' armies.

I am proud to be a marine.

songwriter (song-writ-er): one who writes music or lyrics to songs.

space explorer (space, ex-plor-er): one who travels in space to report new discoveries in space.

spaceman (space-man): one travels in space to observe planets.

speaker (speak-er): one who lectures or speaks on special subjects.

specialist (spe-cial-ist): one who is restricted to one professional or occupation.

speech therapist (speech, ther-a-pist): one who is trained to work with speech disorders caused by physical defects or by mental disorders.

speechwriter (speech-writ-er): one who writes compositions, addresses, and speeches on certain subjects.

sports center (sports, cen-ter): a store that sells sports equipment and sportswears.

Sports center. A store that sells exercise and sports equipments.

sports commentator (sports, com-men-ta-tor): one who writes and discusses sports events.

sporting good store (sport-ing, good, store): a store that sells sporting equipment for boating, fishing, hunting, etc.

sports person (sports, per-son): one who engages and participates in sports.

statistician (stat-is-ti-cian): one who collects and tabulates data.

state trooper (state, troop-er): a police officer that works for the state.

steel engraver (steel, en-grav-er): one who engraves, makes designs on steel.

steelworker (steel-work-er): one who works with steel or factory where steel is made.

stenographer (ste-nog-ra-pher): one who is skilled in writing shorthand.

stockbreeder (stok-breed-er): one who breeds and raises livestock.

stockbroker (stok-bro-ker): one who buys and sells stock and securities.

stock company owner (stok-, com-pa-ny, own-er): one who owns a corporation that issues stock.

stocker (stok-er): one who supplies fuel for locomotive.

stockholder (stok-hold-er): an owner of corporate *stock.*

stockman (stok-man): one who raises livestock; one who works in a stockroom or warehouse.

stone cutter (stone-cut-ter): one who cuts stone.

stonemason (stone-ma-son): one who prepares and lays stone in building.

storage house owner (stor-age, house, own-er): one who charges a fee for keeping storage goods safe for persons.

storekeeper (store-keep-er): one who has charge of a store or owns it.

storyteller (sto-ry-tell-er): one who tells stories for business and pleasure for children and groups.

substitute (sub-sti-tute): a person who takes the place of the working person, a substitute teacher, nurse, or secretary.

sugar farmer (sug-ar, farm-er): one who grows sugarcane to make commercial sugar.

summoner (sum-mon-er): one who summons a person to appear in court.

street cleaner (street, clean-er): one who cleans and sweeps streets debris.

studio worker (stu-dio, work-er): a workroom where filming and broadcasting for radio, TV, motion pictures, and artistic work is done.

stuntman (stunt-man): one who does dangerous acts and stunts in circus, motion pictures, and shows.

superintendent (su-per-in-ten-dent): in charge of supervising schools, companies, and factories, etc.

supermarket owner (su-per-mar-ket, own-er): one who sells food and household supplies.

surf rider (surf rid-er): one who uses a surfboard for surfing.

surgeon (sur-geon): one who practices surgery and performs operation on ill patients.

surveyor (sur-vey-or): one who examines the condition and quality of land.

swimmer (swim-mer): one who swims in water as a sport, or being a teacher or professional.

swimming pool dealer (swim-ming, pool, deal-er): one who makes, sells, or installs swimming pools and its materials.

switchboard operator (switch-board, op-er-a-tor): one who handles connecting telephone calls for business.

switchman (switch-man): one who switches for railroad.

symbolist (sym-bol-ist): one who interprets meaning of symbols in art, science, and math.

T

tailor (tai-lor): one who makes or repairs clothes to fit persons.

tallyman (tal-ly-man): one who keeps count of numbers, volume, and votes.

tanning shop (tan-ning, shop): a shop to tan (make brown or darken) the body under lights.

tap dancer (tap, danc-er): one who dances in shoes by tapping the floor with the heels and toes.

tapster (tap-ster): a bartender.

taster (tast-er): one who tastes foods and liquid to ensure good quality.

tattoo shop (tat-too, shop): a shop that draws, writes, and makes designs on a person's body.

tax preparation man (tax, pre-pa-ra-tion, man): one who prepares tax forms.

taxi driver (taxi, driv-er): a licensed automobile driver who charges passengers a fare to pick up and take them to places in cities and towns.

teacher (teach-er): one who teaches students in schools, colleges, universities, and homes.

technician (tech-ni-cian): one who specializes in handling instruments in performing tasks.

technologist (tech-nol-o-gist): one who has knowledge of industry and how things are produced.

tennis player (ten-nis, play-er): a player of a game that is played by striking the ball back and forth with a racket over a net stretched between two players on a court.

telephone operator (tele-phone, op-er-a-tor): one who assists a person on the telephone system for communication.

television personality (tele-vi-sion, per-son-al-i-ty): one in charge of TV programs, as a host or announcer.

termite technician (ter-mite, tech-ni-cian): one who is skilled in destroying pests and small insects.

timekeeper (time-keep-er): one who keeps time for games, work, or races.

tinner (tin-ner): one who makes cans and tin for storage and other services.

tire dealer (tire, deal-er): one who sells tires or wheels for vehicles for all kinds of transportation.

tobacco farmer (to-bac-co, farm-er): a farmer who grows tobacco for chewing and smoking.

toll keeper (toll, keep-er): one who collects toll fees at the entrance of bridges and roads.

toolmaker (tool-mak-er): one who makes tools.

towing serviceman (tow-ing, ser-vice-man): one who pulls and hauls vehicles for services.

town clerk (town, clerk): an official who keeps records of a town.

toxicologist (tox-i-col-o-gist): one who studies the effects of chemicals on animals, people, and the environment.

trackman (track-man): one who competes in track events as a runner.

tractor dealer (trac-tor, deal-er): one who sells farm equipment for breaking soil and cutting grass.

tradesman (trades-man): one who deals with retail dealers, trailers, mobile home dealers: One who sells or makes temporary or permanent dwellings.

trainer (train-er): one who trains animals and persons to develop skills and performance.

trapper (trap-per): one who traps or catches animals for fur.

travel agent (trav-el, agent): one who arranges travel and accommodation for travels and tourists.

traveling salesman (trav-el-ing, sales-man): one who travels to sell or take orders for business.

translator (trans-la-tor): one who interprets, transforms in writing, spoken language into another form: English language to French.

tree farmer (tree farm-er): one who raises trees for building homes, furniture, and paper uses.

tree surgeon (tree, sur-geon): one who studies treatments and diseases of trees.

treasurer (trea-sur-er): an officer of a state who has charge of funds and revenue.

trooper (troop-er): a state policeman.

truck driver (truck, driv-er): one who drives trucks, delivering supplies and merchandise.

truck farmer (truck, farm-er): one who produces vegetables for the market.

trumpeter (trum-pet-er): one who plays a trumpet.

turfman (turf-man): one who is devoted to horse racing.

tutor (tu-tor): one who teaches privately or gives individual instructions.

tuxedo shop (tux-e-do, shop): a shop that sells or rents attire, formal wear for parties, evening events, and weddings, etc.

typist (typ-ist): one who is skilled in typing.

U

undercover agent (un-der-cov-er, agent): one who engages in spying for secret investigations.

undertaker (un-der-tak-er): one who deals with cremation, burial of the dead and funerals.

unemployment insurance worker (un-em-ploy-ment, in-sur-ance, work-er): one who works with jobless persons, giving benefits in payments or assistances to out-of-work persons.

upholsterer (up-hol-ster-er): one who recovers furniture with fabric and other materials to restore beauty.

umpire (um-pire): one who calls or enforces rules at sports events.

urologist (urol-o-gist): a specialist who deals with the bladder and kidneys.

utility worker (util-i-ty, work-er): one who works for the gas, light, or water company, reading meters and making repairs.

V

vacuum cleaner worker (vac-u-um, clean-er, work-er): one who sells and repairs vacuum cleaners.

vender (vend-er): one who sells as a peddler, small quantities from vehicles, small shops, and windows.

ventriloquist (ven-tril-o-quist): one who provides entertainment by using *ventriloquism,* to carry on an apparent conversation with a hand-manipulated dummy.

veterinarian (vet-er-i-nar-i-an): doctors who treats ill animals.

video engineer (vid-eo, en-gi-neer): one who operates video and television programs.

video shop (vid-eo, shop): a shop that rents movies and video games.

violinist (vi-o-lin-ist): one who plays a violin.

viticulturist (vi-ti-cul-tur-ist): one who studies how to grow grapes.

vocalist (vo-cal-ist): one who sings.

volcanologist (vol-ca-nol-o-gist): one who studies how volcanoes are formed and their behavior.

voodooist (voo-doo-ist): one who practices the religion of voodoo; one who uses witchcraft, charms, and casts spells.

W

waiter (wait-er): one who serves food and drinks in restaurants.

waitress (wait-ress): a female who serves food and drink in restaurants.

wallpaper hanger (wall-pa-per hang-er): one who hangs wallpaper as covering for walls and ceilings of rooms.

warden (war-den): the chief officer for prisons.

warder (ward-er): a keeper, guard, or watchman for persons in confinement or penitentiary.

ware house man (ware-house-man): one who works or owns a place where goods and merchandise are stored.

warrantor (war-ran-tor): one who makes or gives warranty to another.

washer woman (wash-er-wom-an): one who does laundry.

watch maker (watch-mak-er): one who makes or repairs watches.

watch man (watch-man): one who keeps watch or guards over buildings, day or night.

water distributor (wa-ter, dis-trib-u-tor): one who sells fresh bottled water for business.

water man (wa-ter-man): one who works or lives on the *water*. A man who makes his living from the *water* by fishing.

weather man (weath-er-man): one who tells the weather conditions.

weaver (weav-er): one who weaves textiles.

welder (weld-er): one who joins pieces of metal together.

weight control center (weight, con-trol, cen-ter): a building or room to exercise, watch, and restrain food intake for weight loss.

welfare worker (wel-fare, work-er): one who works for the government to improve the social and economic condition of needy persons.

whaler (whal-er): one who hunts whales in whaleboats.

wharfinger (wharf-in-ger): one who keeps a wharf for landing goods for a fee.

wheat farmer (wheat, farm-er): one who raises grain for bread, cereal and provides flour for most pastries.

wheel chair provider (wheel-chair, pro-vid-er): one who makes or sells mobile chairs for disabled persons. Chairs for persons with limited walking abilities.

wicker worker (wick-er-work-er): one who works with making baskets; one who weaves twigs into other art crafts.

wig dealer (wig, deal-er): one who makes or sells artificial hair for covering the head.

wild life and forestry worker (wild-life and for-est-ry work-er): one skilled in knowledge of wild animals, trees, and plants.

window dresser (win-dow, dress-er): one who arranges and designs attractive windows for business with art or writing.

window tinter (win-dow, tint-er): one who shades or screens windows to regulate lights on windows.

window washer (win-dow, wash-er): one who cleans and washes windows.

wine grower (wine, grow-er): one who grows fruits for making wine.

wire worker (wire-work-er): one who manufactures articles from wire.

wood crafter (wood-craft-er): one skilled in constructing articles made of wood.

wood cutter (wood-cut-ter): one who cuts or chops wood.

wood engraver (wood-en-grav-er): one who designs figures and letters on wood surfaces.

wool grower (wool-grow-er): one who raises sheep for wool.

working man (work-ing-man): a male labor worker.

working woman (work-ing-wom-an): a female labor worker.

wreath maker (wreath, mak-er): one who makes wreaths for home decorations, graves, etc.

wrecker (wreck-er): one who tears down and removes old buildings.

wrecker service (wreck-er ser-vice): one who pulls buildings or carry wrecks and broken-down vehicles away.

wrestler (wres-tler): someone who engages in wrestling.

writer (writ-er): one who writes books, articles and stories.

X

x-ray technician (x-ray tech-ni-cian): one who is trained to take x-ray photographs.

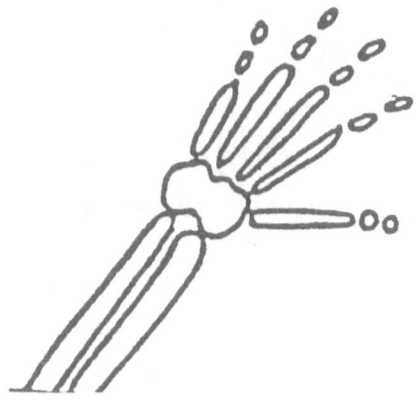

What would an x-ray technician make?

xylophonist (xy-lo-phon-ist): one who plays a music instrument with rows of wooden bars and mallets.

Y

yardman (yard-man): a man employed to do work over the yard; or a sailor who works on the yard.

yardmaster (yard-mas-ter): a railroad official in charge of a yard.

yachtsman (yachts-man): one who owns or sails a yacht.

Daily the yachtsman have fun.

yarn seller (yarn sell-er): one who sells yarns, needles, looms, and knitting materials, etc.

yeoman (yeo-man): a petty officer in the U.S. Navy, who performs clerical duties.

yogurt seller (yo-gurt, sell-er): one who sell yogurt. A curled thicked milk treated with bacteria for healthy eating.

youth center director (youth, cen-ter, di-rec-tor): a manager of a center where young people are trained in special skills through recreation, counseling, and workshops.

Z

zookeeper (zoo-keep-er): one who protects and cares for zoo animals.

Animals at the zoo.

zoologist (zo-ol-o-gist): one who studies animal classification and development.
zoning consultant (zon-ing, con-sul-tant): a person that gives advice on city and town divisions into zones.

Activities At School and Home

for young persons 5-11 years of age.

1. *Invite resources people, such as clothing buyer, dentist, doctor, nurse, or farmer to talk to the pupil about their job responsibilities.*

2. *Have pupils compile a scrapbook containing pictures of various occupations performed in your town.*

3. *Have pupils make a list of their aspirations for future jobs.*

4. *Show filmstrips or videos about different careers.*

5. *Have students identify some of the lowest and the highest paying jobs.*

6. *Have a career day at school. Pupils dress up for different kinds of occupations.*

7. *Fill a box with various careers. Ask pupil to choose a career from the box and tell about the career.*

8. *Make a list of likes and dislikes about serveral careers.*

9. *Assign pupils to report about different careers.*

10. *Discuss education and training skills for certain careers.*

11. *If possible, take vacations to learn about other jobs in various places of the world.*

12. *Speak to people in the field you're considering entering.*

Twenty Things That Matters Most
for young persons 12-18 years of age.

1. Shoot for the moon, even if you miss it, you will land among the stars.
2. If you can imagine it, you can achieve it. If you dream it, you can become it.
3. The future belongs to those who believe in the beauty of their dream.
4. No one who gave his best ever regretted it.
5. People don't go to work to acquire, they go to work to become.
6. A great pleasure in life is doing what people say you cannot do.
7. Opportunity is missed by most peope because it is dressed in overalls and looked like work.
8. Strong lives are motivated by dynamic purpose.
9. Nothing great comes without a price.
10. Conquer every hill, every mountain, and setback that tries to defeat you.
11. The best jobs come from the heart. It may require some sacrifices.
12. Nothing stops the man who desires to achieve.
13. You have the key to happiness and success yourself.
14. Whatever you dream about, you can become.
15. Don't wait for your ship to come in, swim out to it.
16. Don't hide your gifts under a basket. Use what you have.
17. Balance learning with work and fun.

18. Education should prepare people not just to earn a living but to live a life, a creative, humane and sensitive life.
19. Spectacular achievement is always preceded by spectacular preparation.
20. The key to victory is a will to win.

To order additional books
Contact Delois Pippen
P.O. Box 129
Hamburg, Arkansas 71646
Phone # 870-853-5065